The Hogwarts Exp
Meals Straight from the Food-Cart

Magical Meals and Treats to Enjoy on Your Way to Hogwarts

by

P.D. Morgan

Copyright Notes

Table of Contents

Introduction

Sure, the Hogwarts Express may be a magical train that leaves from platform 9¾, but that doesn't mean you'll arrive at Hogwarts in seconds like a Japanese bullet train. To be honest, we're not sure if it can't or if Dumbledore just prefers for his students to appreciate the landscapes on their way to Hogwarts - but either is fine by us because that means there's more time to splurge and feast on the food cart meals and treats served during the ride!

With The Hogwarts Express: Meals Straight from the Food-Cart, you'll find and make some amazing magical recipes fit for half-bloods, witches, and wizards on their way to Hogwarts for the school year. Harry and his friends may have started as eleven years old who were primarily drawn to the train's candies and desserts, but as they got older, they also got much hungrier. That meant they started exploring The Hogwarts Express' full menu: appetizers, mains, drinks, AND desserts.

With more than enough time over the years to try every dish and treat served on the train, we've gathered their favorite ones in this cookbook! We may not be able to find you a seat on the train (unless you can get past the wall on the platform), but we certainly can share the incredible journey our favorite wizards are on through their favorite foods!

The acceptance letters have already been mailed out for this year's class, hence our current train ride to Hogwarts - but don't be discouraged. You can always try again next year! In the meantime, why not treat yourself to some Quidditch Popcorn Brooms, Half Moon Pasties, Polyjuice Potion, or some Golden Snitch Pops? We've got lots to choose from!

HHHHHHHHHHHHHHHHHHHHHHHHHHHHHHHHHHHHHHHHH

Magical Drink Recipes

HHHHHHHHHHHHHHHHHHHHHHHHHHHHHHHHHHHHHHH

(1) Butterbeer

Arguably, this is the most popular drink in the wizard world. It is generally served warm and in mugs, with a delicious foam at the top!

Ingredient List:

- 2 liters of Cream Soda
- 6 tablespoons butter
- 4 tablespoons brown sugar
- 10 Werther's Original candies
- 1 ½ cup heavy cream

HHHHHHHHHHHHHHHHHHHHHHHHHHHHHHHHHHHHHHHHHH

How to Cook:

Melt butter and brown sugar together in the microwave, stir and set aside

Pour cream soda into a pot and bring to a light boil

Add in sugar and butter mixture to the boiling soda, and stir to mix

Add in the heavy cream and Werther's candies, stir until candies have melted

Use a ladle to fill coffee cups ¾ way

Relax and enjoy!

(2) Pumpkin Juice

Pumpkin Juice is another widely popular drink in the wizard world.

Ingredient List:

- 32 oz apple juice
- 15 oz pumpkin puree
- 10 oz apricot nectar
- 1 teaspoon vanilla extract
- 2 teaspoons pumpkin pie spice
- Optional- 1 teaspoon ginger

HHHHHHHHHHHHHHHHHHHHHHHHHHHHHHHHHHHHHHHHH

How to Cook:

In a large pot, combine the apple juice and pumpkin puree, and bring to a boil

Add in apricot nectar and continue boiling for 5 minutes, stirring occasionally

Add in vanilla extract and pumpkin pie spice and continue boiling for 5 minutes, stirring occasionally

Reduce to simmer for 20 minutes

Ladle into coffee mugs and enjoy!

(3) Wolfsbane Potion

A potion that relieves the symptoms of lycanthropy (turning into a werewolf). This is the potion Professor Lupin takes in Prisoner of Azkaban.

Ingredient List:

- 1.25 oz Whiskey
- 1.25 oz bitter liquor
- 1 cup coke

HHHHHHHHHHHHHHHHHHHHHHHHHHHHHHHHHHHHHHHHHHH

How to Cook:

Mix all ingredients together (whiskey, then bitter liquor, then coke)

Enjoy and hope you don't turn into a werewolf!

(4) Patronus Punch

One of the most advanced forms of magic, a patronus is a magical shield between the witch/wizard and a Dementor. Each witch/wizard's patronus will take the form of a specific animal. Harry was taught how to conjure a patronus by Professor Lupin in the Prisoner of Azkaban. Harry's patronus is a stag.

Ingredient List:

- 1 liter tonic water
- 2 liter Sprite
- 2 cups limeade
- 2 cups vodka
- 1 or 2 glow green glow sticks

HHHHHHHHHHHHHHHHHHHHHHHHHHHHHHHHHHHHHHHH

How to Cook:

Mix together all ingredients in a large punch bowl.

Clean and then activate glow sticks.

Gently drop glow sticks into the punch (do not puncture glowsticks).

Turn off the lights and enjoy!

(5) Amortentia

The most potent love potion, not a single drinker can resist its effects. In book/move #6, Half-Blood Prince, Ron accidentally ate the chocolates that Romilda Vane and tried to trick Harry with so he would take her to Professor Slughorn's Christmas Party.

Ingredient List:

- 3 cups Aperol or Campari
- 2 cups gin
- 4 cups pomegranate juice
- 2 bottles sparkling rose wine
- 2 heart-shaped ice cube trays
- 12 strawberries, halved
- 1 cup pomegranate seeds

HHHHHHHHHHHHHHHHHHHHHHHHHHHHHHHHHHHHHHHHH

How to Cook:

Freeze halved strawberries and pomegranate seeds in ice cube trays overnight.

Mix Aperol, gin, pomegranate juice, and sparking rose together in a large punch bowl.

Add in strawberry/pomegranate ice cubes.

(6) Polyjuice Potion

Polyjuice Potion allows a witch or wizard to turn into another person temporarily. All they must have is a part of the body from the other person (In the Chamber of Secrets, Hermione accidentally uses cat hair instead of Millicent Bulstrode's hair and ends up assuming cat-like features). Polyjuice potion allows the users to turn change appearance but not species.

Ingredient List:

- 2 liters of Sprite
- ½ gallon lime sherbet
- Green food coloring

HHHHHHHHHHHHHHHHHHHHHHHHHHHHHHHHHHHHHHHH

How to Cook:

Pour Sprite into a large punch bowl.

Add in a few drops of green food coloring to intensify the green color.

Add in lime sherbet one scoop at a time.

Enjoy your magical drink!

(7) Witches Brew

A drink sold at many pubs in the wizarding world, witches brew is similar to a Guinness. A thick stout with a large foam head.

Ingredient List:

- 1 liter ginger ale
- 1 cup vodka
- ½ cup water
- ½ cup sugar
- 10 kiwi fruit, peeled
- Handful of fresh mint

HHHHHHHHHHHHHHHHHHHHHHHHHHHHHHHHHHHHHHHHHH

How to Cook:

Boil sugar and water in a saucepan on the stove, stir until sugar is dissolved, remove from heat, and place in refrigerator to cool for 10-20 minutes.

In a blender, purée kiwi, sugar mixture, and mint (if not cold enough, add a few ice cubes and re-blend).

Pour into a small punch bowl and add in ginger ale and vodka.

Enjoy and cast some spells!

(8) Goblet of Fire Cocktail

The Goblet of Fire is a large wooden cup used to select participants from each house for the Triwizard Tournament. It is supposed only to allow participants 17 years old and older to enter the tournament. Still, somehow in the 4th movie/book The Goblet of Fire, someone managed to transfix the Goblet and enter Harry's name into the tournament. Once the Goblet chose the participants, there was no way for them to back out of the tournament.

Ingredient List:

- 1.25 oz vodka
- 1.25 oz blue curacao
- 5 oz lemonade
- Splash of Fireball
- Dash of cinnamon

HHHHHHHHHHHHHHHHHHHHHHHHHHHHHHHHHHHHHHHHHH

How to Cook:

Mix together vodka, blue curacao, lemonade, and fireball.

Light on fire.

Sprinkle Cinnamon in flames for added effect.

Can you stand the test? Enjoy!

Do not consume flames

(9) Unicorn Blood

A unicorn is the purest creature there is in the magical world. Killing one is considered the ultimate crime. Drinking the blood of the unicorn will keep you alive, but at a terrible price. The drinker of unicorn blood will survive but only live a half-life. In the Sorcerer's Stone, Harry and his friends come across unicorn blood for the first time while on detention with Hagrid in the Forbidden Forest.

Ingredient List:

- 2 tablespoons raspberry purée
- Peach vodka
- Dash of gold dust

HHHHHHHHHHHHHHHHHHHHHHHHHHHHHHHHHHHHHHHHHH

How to Cook:

Mix together the peach vodka and gold dust, and this creates a shimmery liquor.

Pour vodka mixture into a martini glass, about ¾ way full.

Add in 2 tablespoons of the raspberry puree.

Watch the magic unfold and enjoy!

(10) Felix Felicis

Though hard to make, this potion brings the drinker good luck! If made wrong, the consequences are disastrous.

Ingredient List:

- Champagne
- ¼ oz simple syrup
- 1 ½ oz ginger beer

HHHHHHHHHHHHHHHHHHHHHHHHHHHHHHHHHHHHHHHHHH

How to Cook:

Add simple syrup to the bottom of a champagne flute and top with ginger beer.

Complete remaining portion with champagne.

Enjoy!

Magical Appetizer Recipes

HHHHHHHHHHHHHHHHHHHHHHHHHHHHHHHHHHHHHHHHHHH

(11) Fried Howlers

Generally, we all know when someone is mad at us. No one likes being yelled at. Now imagine being at school and receiving a red letter that SCREAMS at you in the person's voice! And when the message is over, the envelope bursts into flames. Everyone from Neville Longbottom to Ron Weasley, Hermione to Harry's Aunt Petunia all received Howler's.

Ingredient List:

- 12 wonton wrappers
- 1 egg
- 8 oz crème cheese
- 16 oz Strawberry Preserves or Pumpkin Puree
- 1 tablespoon water
- Vegetable or Canola Oil
- Small cake decorating gel- black
- Small cake decorating gel- red
- Fill a medium pot ½ way with oil and heat to 350°F.

HHHHHHHHHHHHHHHHHHHHHHHHHHHHHHHHHHHHHHHHHH

How to Cook:

Mix together the crème cheese, and strawberry preserves in a bowl until you have reached a marbled consistency (option to use crème cheese and pumpkin puree); set bowl aside.

Lay each wonton wrapper, point facing up, so you have a diamond shape, and place 1-2 tablespoons of filling in the center.

Dip finger in water and trace along edges of wonton wrapper.

To create envelope shape: fold side corners in, then bottom corner up, then top corner down.

Lightly press edges together to create a seal (retrace edges of wonton wrapper with water if needed).

Gently add a few wonton wrappers at a time to the oil, and fry until golden brown; this should take no more than a few minutes.

Use a spoon to remove fried wonton wrappers and place them on a cookie rack to cool. Repeat with remaining wonton wrappers.

Once cool, use black decorative gel to draw two lines for eyes and the red decorative gel to draw lips.

Arrange on a plate and enjoy!

(12) Herbology Bites

Herbology class at Hogwarts was no typical biology lesson. It was hands-on and had the potential to be very dangerous. From harvesting Mandrakes (whose screams can kill you), spotting the difference between Devil's Snare and Flitterbloom (one is deadly, one is harmless), to knowing the benefits of Gillyweed and Dittany, Herbology was a genuine introduction for many young wizards into the magical world around them.

Ingredient List:

- French Baguette
- 8 oz Cream Cheese
- 2 cucumbers
- Chives
- Paprika

HHHHHHHHHHHHHHHHHHHHHHHHHHHHHHHHHHHHHHHHHHHHHHH

How to Cook:

Thinly slice baguette (about a quarter inch to a half inch slices); arrange on a plate and set aside.

Thinly slice cucumber; set aside.

Spread a small amount of cream cheese on each slice of bread and top with cucumber.

Sprinkle chives and paprika on top.

Enjoy your garden plate!

(13) Wizard Hats

One of the most famous objects in Harry was The Sorting Hat. Containing the intelligence of the four founders, The Sorting Hat was placed on First Year's heads and able to see into their magical capabilities. It would use its mastery of Legilimency to sort the First Years into their houses.

Ingredient List:

- 1 box pie crust (optional: crescent roll dough)
- 2 tablespoons sugar
- 1 tablespoon cinnamon
- Miniature chocolate chips

HHHHHHHHHHHHHHHHHHHHHHHHHHHHHHHHHHHHHHHHHHH

How to Cook:

Heat oven to 375°F.

If using pie crust- unroll pie crust and cut into 12-16 wedges.

If using crescent rolls- unroll each individual roll.

Spoon a small amount of mini-cholate chips (0.5 teaspoons- 1 teaspoon worth) on the wide end of each wedge.

Starting at the wide end, roll up each edge just enough to cover the chocolate chips.

Place each hat onto an ungreased baking sheet.

Mix Sugar and Cinnamon together in a bowl and sprinkle over each hat.

Optional- bend and twist the small pointy end of each hat to give a more realistic look.

Bake until golden brown (10-12 minutes).

Cool on a cookie rack.

(14) Ollivander's Pretzel Wand

Garrick Ollivander is the owner of Ollivander's wand shop in Diagon Alley. Known as the best wandmaker globally, Wizards and Witches would travel from all over to buy from him. Ollivander is even quoted as saying, "I remember every wand I have ever sold." Each wand would be made of a special wood with a core such as a phoenix feather or unicorn hair and would bring out the best power from each Witch or Wizard. The wand chooses the Wizard.

Ingredient List:

- 24 pretzel rods
- Multi-colored sprinkles
- Mini M&Ms
- Crushed Oreos
- Crushed peanuts
- Any other assorted toppings
- Different colored melting chocolate (can be found at a local craft store)
- Large heatproof cups (to hold melted chocolate- makes dipping the pretzel easier!)

HHHHHHHHHHHHHHHHHHHHHHHHHHHHHHHHHHHHHHHHHH

How to Cook:

Arrange assorted toppings into their bowls; set aside.

Melting chocolates can either be melted on the stove or in a microwave bowl.

Pour melted chocolate into heatproof cups.

Dip pretzel rods into chocolate and sprinkle with various toppings.

Set on cookie rack to cool.

**There are endless possibilities for decorating the wands! You can even drizzle one color of chocolate onto another. Have fun! **

(15) Deviled Dragon Eggs

Dragon eggs are a prized possession and considered a non-tradeable material by the Ministry of Magic. They are highly protected by their mothers and require a lot of heat. Our first introduction to dragons in Harry is during First Year when Hagrid won a dragon egg off a "cloaked stranger" at the Hog's Head pub in Hogsmead. Harry, Ron, and Hermione were all in Hagrid's cabin when Norbert hatched.

Ingredient List:

- 1 dozen eggs
- Vinegar
- Food Coloring
- Cups of Coffee Mugs (to hold the different colored dye)
- 1 Large bowl (for yolks)
- Mayo
- Mustard
- (optional) 3 Ziploc Bags or Icing Piping Bags
- (optional) 3 Small Bowls

HHHHHHHHHHHHHHHHHHHHHHHHHHHHHHHHHHHHHHHHH

How to Cook:

Place the eggs in a medium to a large-sized pot.

Cover with cold water.

Place pan on the stove and bring the water to a rapid boil; continue boiling for approximately 5 minutes.

Turn off heat and let the eggs be in hot water for about 10 minutes.

Drain cold water out of the pan and run cold water over the eggs till they are cool to the touch.

While eggs are cooling, distribute 1 tablespoon of vinegar and several drops of food coloring into each cup (one color per cup).

The full remainder of the cups is halfway with water (enough to cover the egg when placed in the cup).

Before placing an egg in a cup, lightly roll the egg on the counter to create small cracks in the shell- DO NOT PEEL THE EGG YET!

Place eggs in cups and let sit for a few minutes.

If you have any leftover egg dying kits from Easter, these can be substituted for the food coloring

Gently use a spoon to lift the eggs out of the cups; leave the eggs in the dye solution for a few more minutes if you want a darker color.

Let the eggs sit for a couple of minutes on a paper towel before peeling (this helps the color set in).

Peel the eggs---the crackled coloring looks incredible, doesn't it?!?!

Cut the eggs in half lengthwise and place yolks in a bowl.

Mix in preferred amounts of Mayo and Mustard with yolk until you have reached a creamy consistency.

(Optional)- Divide yolk mixture between the small bowls and add 3-5 drops of food coloring into each; stir to achieve a marbled look.

(Optional)- Scoop yolk mixture into individual Ziplock bags and cut off a small section of the corner.

Arrange dyed egg whites on a plate and pipe in the (colored) yolk mixture.

Enjoy!

(16) Yorkshire Pudding

Yorkshire Pudding was a staple of the Hogwart's Sunday dinners. It is typically served with Roast Beef. If you look carefully, you can see Yorkshire Pudding in almost all of the films.

Ingredient List:

- 2 cups milk
- 4 eggs
- 2 1/2 cups flour
- 1/4 cup vegetable oil

HHHHHHHHHHHHHHHHHHHHHHHHHHHHHHHHHHHHHHHHHH

How to Cook:

Heat oven to 425°F.

Whisk together milk and eggs in a large bowl.

Add in flour a half cup at a time, whisk until well blended (if it froths, that is ok); set aside.

Place approx. 1 teaspoon of oil into each section of a muffin tin and place on the top shelf of the oven for about 5 minutes (if it smokes, that is ok).

Remove from oven and spoon approx. ¼ cup of batter into each muffin cup (cup should be approx. ¾ full).

Bake until golden brown (approx. 20 minutes).

Serve immediately (Don't open the oven before serving, or else the puddings may collapse).

Enjoy!

(17) Monster Books

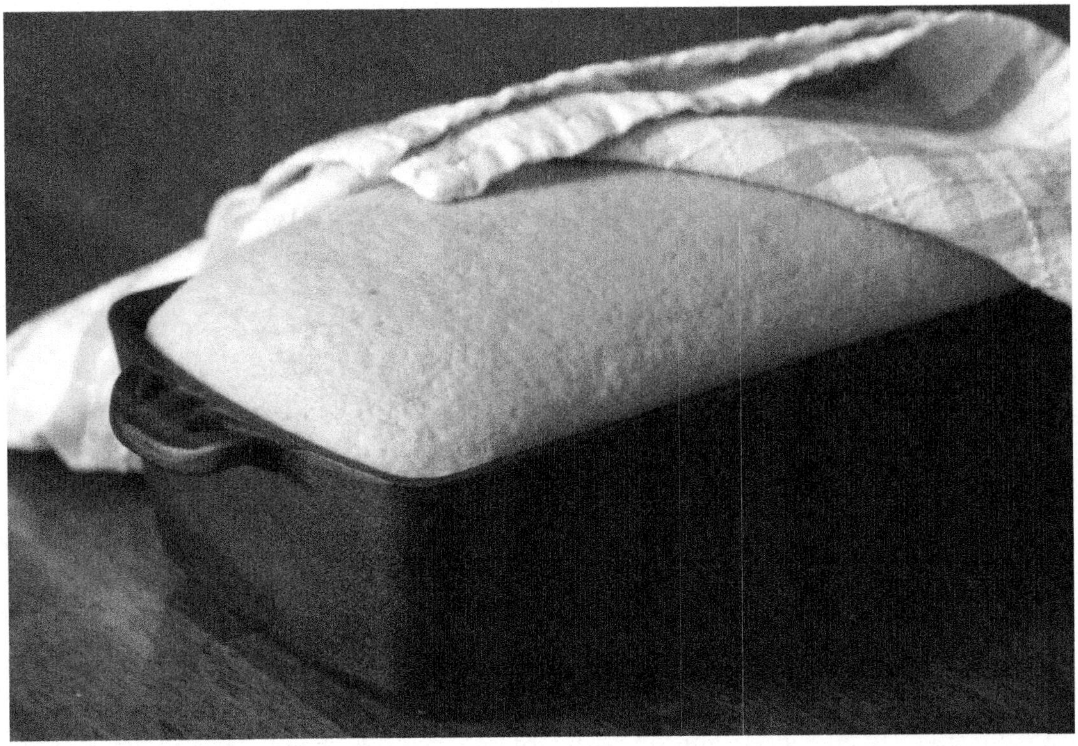

Hagrid gifted a required book for all Third Years, Harry his copy. The book contains what you need to know about taking care of magical creatures, but the book is highly volatile and often attacks whoever is trying to read it. When Harry opens his copy, the book attempted to attack his hand, and Harry Has to use a belt to keep it shut.

Ingredient List:

- Loaf of bread (approx. 24 slices)
- 12 slices of cheese
- 12 slices of meat
- 24 green olives (with pits)
- 24 toothpicks
- 1 cup

HHHHHHHHHHHHHHHHHHHHHHHHHHHHHHHHHHHHHHHHHH

How to Cook:

Place cup on each piece of bread and press down to create a circle indent.

Using a knife, cut out each indent and place the circle bread piece aside.

Repeat for all 24 slices.

Using a knife, cut the jagged edge into pieces of cheese and meat (this will end up being the monster teeth).

Repeat for all slices of meat and cheese.

Place one circle piece of bread on the bottom and arrange 1 slice of meat and 1 slice of cheese on top, top with another piece of bread.

Repeat for the remaining slices of bread, cheese, and meat.

Once all sandwiches have been constructed, place too green olives on the edge of the sandwich top and secure using toothpicks.

Enjoy your library of Monsters!

(18) Hogs Mead BBQ Cornish Balls

Hogsmead is a secret all wizard village favored by many. During their Third Year, students are allowed to visit Hogsmead on the weekend (many go to get candies from Honeydukes or visit the Shrieking Shack). Because Harry ran away from his aunt and uncle, he has no guardian to sign the permission slip and therefore is not allowed to go. Harry originally mopes around the castle until he runs into the Weasley Twins, who present him with the Marauder's Map. Harry Uses this map and his invisibility cloak to sneak into Hogsmead.

Ingredient List:

- Bag of frozen meatballs (approx. 1.5-2 lbs.)
- 18oz containers of BBQ sauce
- 2 cups jelly of your choice

HHHHHHHHHHHHHHHHHHHHHHHHHHHHHHHHHHHHHHHHHH

How to Cook:

Mix BBQ sauce and jelly in a bowl.

Toss in frozen meatballs and stir till covered.

Pour coated meatballs (and remaining sauce) into crockpot.

Cook on high for 3 ½ hours.

Serve in a bowl or stick each individual meatball with a toothpick.

Enjoy!

(19) Argog's Nest

Argog is an Acromantula (an enormously large spider with a taste for humans and potent but sought after venom). Hagrid raised Argog from an egg and later gave him a home in the Forbidden Forest. Argog is loyal to Hagrid but Hagrid alone. We first meet Argog in Book 2, *The Chamber of Secrets*, when Hagrid tells Ron and Harry to "follow the spiders." Ron and Harry follow the spiders into the Forbidden Forest only to find themselves in a massive nest of spiders.

Ingredient List:

- 2 sleeves of Ritz crackers
- Peanut butter
- Mini-pretzel sticks
- Box of raisins
- (Optional)- Poppyseeds

HHHHHHHHHHHHHHHHHHHHHHHHHHHHHHHHHHHHHHHHHHH

How to Cook:

Arrange one sleeve of Ritz crackers on a baking sheet.

Smooth approx. 1 tablespoon of peanut butter onto each cracker.

Place six mini-pretzel sticks halfway onto each cracker; three on each side.

Using the second sleeve of crackers, place another cracker on top of the first.

Take two raisins and place them on the edge of the cracker sandwich; these are the eyes.

(Optional) sprinkle with poppy seeds for extra effect.

Enjoy your spider's nest!

(20) Quidditch Popcorn Brooms

Quidditch is a trendy game throughout the Wizard World. Harry even becomes the youngest seeker ever allowed to join the Gryffindor Quidditch Team. Professor McGonagall gifted Harry a Nimbus 2000 in the 1st book/movie- Harry and the Sorcerer's Stone.

Ingredient List:

- 12 pretzel rods
- 12 brown paper bags
- 6 bags of popped popcorn
- Twine
- Scissors

How to Cook:

Use scissors to cut long thin slits from the top of the bag to three quarters down the bag; repeat this for each bag (the goal is to have the bag look like it has snakes all around its top).

Place a few cups of popcorn into each bag.

Gather loose ends of each bag in one hand and place a pretzel rod down the middle.

Secure the top of the bag with twine (leaving about an inch or two).

Repeat with all bags till you have a broom closet full!

Magical Main Course Recipes

HHHHHHHHHHHHHHHHHHHHHHHHHHHHHHHHHHHHHHHH

(21) Forbidden Forest Feast

The Forbidden Forest is on the edge of the Hogwarts property. The forest is off-limits to students as many powerful and dangerous creatures call the forest home. The forest is home to a herd of Centaurs who come to the aid of Harry and his friends while they are in the forest.

Ingredient List:

- 1 uncooked chicken
- 1 stick butter, diced
- 2 tablespoons butter whole
- Italian seasoning
- Salt
- Pepper
- 3 carrots, peeled
- 3 sticks celery
- 4-6 ears of corn, cut in half
- 4 baking potatoes
- Sour cream
- Chives

HHHHHHHHHHHHHHHHHHHHHHHHHHHHHHHHHHHHHHHH

How to Cook:

Heat oven to 400°F.

Shuck and clean ears of corn set aside.

Scrub potatoes to remove dirt, poke all over with a fork, wrap in foil, set aside.

Rinse chicken and pat dry with a paper towel.

Distribute diced pieces of butter under the skin.

Place carrots and celery inside the body of the chicken and place the chicken in a roasting pan.

Rub outside the chicken with olive oil and then season with salt, pepper, and Italian seasoning.

Roast for 45 minutes, then add baked potatoes to the oven for an additional 30 minutes.

Cut the thickest part of the thigh, and if the liquid runs clear, the chicken is done baking.

Remove baked potatoes from the oven and allow them to sit for several minutes before removing the foil.

Boil a large pot of water on the stove and gently add ears of corn.

Cook corn for only 3-4 minutes.

Remove corn from water and rub with remaining 2 tablespoons of butter, season with salt and pepper.

Place in serving dish and set aside.

Remove potatoes from foil and arrange on serving platter.

Cut slits down the center of potatoes and press open.

Season potatoes with a bit of salt and pepper.

Top with sour cream and chives.

Cut up chicken into sections and arrange on the serving platter: legs, white meat, dark meat.

Bring corn platter, baked potato platter, and chicken platter to the table.

Enjoy!

(22) House Elf Stew

House elves are small creatures with big eyes and shabby, dirty clothing. They are bound to the families they serve, doing everything from cooking to cleaning. We first meet Dobby (the Malfoy's house elf) and are later introduced to Kreacher (the Black's house elf) in the Order of the Phoenix. Kreacher was thought to be both the most miserable house elf of the series and the best cook. He eventually became fond of Harry and cooked him satisfying but straightforward dishes. His two most famous were House Elf Stew and French Onion Soup.

Ingredient List:

- 1 lb. meat of your choice, cut into chunks (NOT GROUND)
- 3 cups broth (vegetable or meat)
- 1 large onion diced
- 1 cup carrots diced
- ½ cup celery diced
- ½ cup frozen peas
- 2 small brown potatoes diced, skins on
- 2 small red potatoes diced, skins on
- 1 cup and 2 Tablespoons flour
- 6 Tablespoons butter, diced (keep cold)
- 3 Tablespoons milk
- 1 tablespoon minced garlic
- Vegetable or olive oil
- 1 teaspoon each of the following:
- Baking powder
- Salt
- Pepper
- Italian seasoning

HHHHHHHHHHHHHHHHHHHHHHHHHHHHHHHHHHHHHHHHHHH

How to Cook:

<u>Stew</u>

Heat oil in a pot and brown meat for two minutes on each side, remove meat from bowl and set aside; DO NOT DRAIN.

In the same pot, add in the diced potatoes and onions and cook until potatoes soften.

Add in carrots, celery, frozen peas, and minced garlic, cook for 2 minutes.

Little by little, add in the 2 Tablespoons flour until all vegetables are coated.

Add in the 3 cups of broth and simmer.

Continue simmering for 30 minutes.

Prepare dumplings (can be made in advance or while the stew is simmering).

After simmering for 30 minutes, add the meat mixture back into stew and stir.

Gently add the dough balls to the mixture with a ladle. The dough should cover the top of the stew.

Let the stew and dough mixture cook for another 10-15 minutes or until dough is puffed up.

Divide the stew and dumplings into individual bowls and enjoy!

Dumplings

Whisk together the remaining 1 cup flour, baking powder, salt, pepper, Italian seasoning.

In a separate bowl, whisk together the egg and milk, set aside.

With your hands, mix the chilled butter into the dry mixture until everything is incorporated.

Slowly pour the milk and butter into the dry mixture and stir until everything is incorporated. If the dough is too sticky, add more flour.

Pull off small sections of the dough and roll into a ball. Think half the size of a golf ball.

Place all dough balls on a plate in preparation for going into the stew.

(23) Fleur Delacour's Bouillabaisse

Fleur Delcaour was a witch from Beauxbatons Academy of Magic, and we met her during the Triwizard Tournament in The Goblet of Fire (movie/book #4). She was the runner-up to Cedric Diggory and later married Bill Weasley (the oldest Weasley Brothers).

Ingredient List:

- Meat
- 1 ½ lbs. red fish cut into large sections (i.e., snapper or salmon)
- 1 ½ lbs. white fish cut into large sections (i.e., haddock or cod)
- 12 jumbo shrimp, de-veined
- 10 large scallops
- 1 lb. mussels
- 1 lb. clams
- ½ lb. squid rings
- Optional- ½ lb. lobster meat
- 2 cans spicy diced tomatoes
- 1 can regular diced tomatoes
- 2 cans stewed tomatoes
- 1 cup white wine
- 3 tablespoons minced garlic
- 3 chicken bouillon cubes or 1 ½ tablespoons powdered chicken bouillon
- 10 leaves fresh basil
- Salt
- Pepper
- Shaved Parmesan
- 1 large baguette, sliced

HHHHHHHHHHHHHHHHHHHHHHHHHHHHHHHHHHHHHHHH

How to Cook:

Slice baguette into 1-inch sections and set aside.

Clean and prepare all seafood.

Add canned tomatoes, white wine, garlic, chicken bouillon, salt, and pepper in a large pot.

Bring to a boil and then reduce to a simmer for 15 minutes.

Add all seafood (starting with the fish) and bring to a boil, then reduce to a simmer for 5-10 minutes.

Ladle soup into individual bowls and top with shaved parmesan.

Serve with a slice of baguette on the side.

Enjoy!

(24) Bangers and Mash

Loved by both the muggles and wizard/witches, bangers and mash was a typical dish of Britain.

Ingredient List:

- 8 sausages
- 2.5 cups beef stock
- ½ cup water
- 4 tablespoons vegetable or olive oil
- 1 large onion, sliced
- 2 tablespoons minced garlic
- 3 tablespoons flour
- 3 cups frozen peas
- 1 lb. small red potatoes, cut in half
- 1 cup milk
- ½ cup cheddar cheese

HHHHHHHHHHHHHHHHHHHHHHHHHHHHHHHHHHHHHHHH

How to Cook:

In a large pot, boil red potatoes until soft, drain, and return to pot.

Mash with a fork until potatoes are crumbled. Add in milk and cheese.

Stir until you get a smooth consistency, cover, and set aside.

Add peas and ½ cup water to a small skillet, cook on low for 10 minutes, set aside.

Heat 2 tablespoons oil in a skillet and add sausages.

Cook on medium heat for 10 minutes (or until cooked all the way through).

Remove sausages from the pan and place in a covered bowl.

Heat remaining 2 tablespoons oil in the same skillet and add onions and garlic, cooking until translucent, approx. 5 minutes.

Add in flour and stir till incorporated.

Add 1 cup beef broth and sliced onions, cook for 2 minutes and then add the remaining cups of beef broth.

Stir until the consistency is that of a thick gravy.

Add sausages back in and stir.

Spoon one large spoonful of both mashed potatoes and peas onto a plate and add one sausage.

Enjoy!

(25) Quidditch Pie

Arguably the most popular game on the Wizard World, quidditch pie is full of meat and vegetables. Perfect for fueling up for a tournament or rewarding yourself after a win!

Ingredient List:

- 1 lb. ground turkey
- 1 ½ Tablespoons minced garlic
- 1 small onion diced
- 1 bag frozen carrots and peas
- 1 packet gravy mix
- 1 bag small red potatoes
- 3 Tablespoons butter
- ½ cup milk
- 1 cup shredded cheese

HHHHHHHHHHHHHHHHHHHHHHHHHHHHHHHHHHHHHHHHHHH

How to Cook:

Fill a large pot halfway with water.

Heat until boiling.

Cut potatoes in half and add to water, boil until softened, approx. 15-20 minutes.

Drain water and transfer potatoes to a large bowl to cool.

Heat oven to 350°F.

Make gravy according to packet instructions, set aside.

Mash potatoes in a large bowl, stir in butter and milk until mixture starts becoming smooth, set aside.

In a skillet, brown ground turkey and onion, approx. 7 minutes.

Once the meat is cooked through, add in frozen carrots and peas until they are softened.

Drain any excess oil/water from the pan.

Stir in the gravy until the mixture is well coated.

Transfer mixture to a casserole dish, cover with mashed potatoes.

Sprinkle cheese on top.

Broil in oven for 15-20 minutes, until cheese is melted and has started turning a golden brown.

Let rest 10 minutes before serving.

This meal is perfect after a long game day. Enjoy!

(26) Half Moon Pasties

The moon is significant in the wizard world. It affects everything from certain animals like werewolves to potions like Polyjuice. There were even rumors that the moon's phases were used in the healing process of certain diseases.

Ingredient List:

- 1 packet pie dough
- ½ lb. ground meat of your choice
- 1 small white onion, diced
- 1 small red onion, diced
- 1 small leek, diced
- 1 medium potato, diced
- 2 medium carrots, peeled and diced
- 2 tablespoons butter
- 1 egg
- Italian seasoning
- Salt
- Pepper

HHHHHHHHHHHHHHHHHHHHHHHHHHHHHHHHHHHHHHHHHH

How to Cook:

Heat oven to 375°F.

Melt butter in a skillet and add onions, cook until translucent.

Add in leeks and cook for 5 minutes, then remove from heat.

In a large bowl, combine ½ lb. meat, potato, and carrots.

Add onion and leek mixture to a large bowl and mix till incorporated.

Season with Italian seasoning, salt, and pepper, and set the mixture aside.

Roll out pastry dough and use a wide mouth cup to trace large circles; the more circles, the better, but don't roll the dough below ¼ inch thick.

Scoop a large spoonful into the center of each pastry circle.

Brush edges of the pastry circle with egg wash and fold in half, pinching edges together to seal.

Line half-moon pastry circles on cooking sheet and bake, brush with remaining egg wash, and bake for 35 minutes.

Remove from oven and allow to cool on a cookie rack for 10 minutes.

Serve and enjoy!

(27) Kreacher's French Onion Soup

One of his two best soups, Kreacher, made Harry French onion soup after Harry gifted him the Regulus Black's Locket.

Ingredient List:

- 3 medium onions, sliced thin
- 2 ½ Tablespoons minced garlic
- 1 medium baguette, sliced thick
- 6 tablespoons butter
- 2.5 tablespoons white wine
- 2 ½ tablespoons flour
- ½ cup beef broth
- ½ cup Gruyere Cheese
- ½ cup Parmesan Cheese
- Salt
- Pepper

HHHHHHHHHHHHHHHHHHHHHHHHHHHHHHHHHHHHHHHHHH

How to Cook:

Heat oven to 375°F.

Slice baguette into thick slices, approx. 1 ½ - 2 inches thick, set aside.

In a medium saucepan, melt 4 Tablespoons of butter and add onions.

Sauté onions on high heat for 5 minutes and then reduce to medium heat until browned, approx. 20 minutes.

Add flour and remaining butter to the pan, stir till incorporated.

Scrape the bottom of the pan with a spatula to loosen any butter or onions that may have stuck to the bottom.

Deglaze the pan with the white wine and pour in beef broth.

Bring to a boil for 3 minutes and then reduce to simmer for 10 minutes.

Using a ladle, spoon soup into individual ramekins till they are ¾ full.

Cover soup with ¾ of the cheese and top with a slice of baguette.

Sprinkle remaining cheese on top of the baguette slice and bake in the oven for 15 minutes (until cheese is bubbly and golden brown.

Serve and enjoy!

(28) Chicken Pot Pie

Another staple during the Hogwarts Feasts, chicken pot pie, was a filling and warm meal that was perfect for filling the bellies of the curious and hardworking students.

Ingredient List:

- 6-8 small chicken breasts, cubed or shredded
- 4 cups chicken stock
- 1.5 cups chopped carrots
- 1.5 cup peas
- 3 cups chopped potatoes
- 2 small onions diced
- ¾ cup diced celery
- ½ cup flour
- ½ cup butter
- 1 egg
- 1 ¼ cup milk
- 4 teaspoons Italian seasoning
- 2 Tablespoons lemon juice
- 2 packet pastry dough (you need 2 sheets)

HHHHHHHHHHHHHHHHHHHHHHHHHHHHHHHHHHHHHHHH

How to Cook:

Preheat oven to 350°F.

Roll out pastry dough and fit into a pie dish, set aside.

Add the shredded/cubed chicken, carrots, potatoes, celery, 2.5 teaspoons Italian seasoning, and chicken stock to a large pot, bring to a boil, then simmer for 20 minutes.

Drain all but 2 cups of the liquid, place contents in a large bowl.

Using the same pot, melt the butter and add the onions, cooking the onions until they become translucent, approx. 5 minutes.

Add in the flour and stir till onions are evenly coated (it is ok to add another ¼ flour here if needed).

Str in the reserved chicken stock a half cup at a time. The sauce should be thick and smooth.

Once all reserved stock has been incorporated, add in the milk and simmer for 2 minutes.

Remove from heat and add in lemon juice and the remaining 1.5 teaspoons Italian seasoning.

Return the cooked chicken and vegetables to the pot and stir.

Gently scoop or pour the mixture into the pie dish and allow it to cool for 10 minutes.

Roll out the second sheet of pastry dough and drape it over the pie dish.

Pinch down around the edges of the dough and trim off excess (you may need to brush the pie crust edges with water for them to seal together when pinched).

Brush the top of the pie crust with the egg and make 3 small slits in the center of the pie (so steam can get out).

Bake in the oven for 25 minutes or until golden brown.

Let sit for 10 minutes and then slice and serve.

Enjoy!

*It is optional to use individual ramekins instead of one large pie dish***

(29) Endless Plate of Sandwiches

Transfiguration changes the physical appearance of an object. A very scientific for of magic, transfiguration is thought to be very hard to pull off. Professor McGonagall summoned a plate for Ron and Harry in Year 2 (Harry and the Chamber of Secrets).

Ingredient List:

- 2 loafs white bread
- 2 loafs wheat bread
- 12 slices provolone cheese
- 12 slices cheddar cheese
- 12 slices turkey
- 12 slices chicken
- Lettuce
- Tomatoes, sliced
- Mayo
- Mustard
- Pickles

HHHHHHHHHHHHHHHHHHHHHHHHHHHHHHHHHHHHHHHH

How to Cook:

Place 12 slices of white bread on a serving tray.

Top with one slice of cheese, one slice of meat, lettuce, tomatoes, pickles, and mayo/mustard.

Top with the remaining 12 slices of white bread.

Repeat for wheat bread.

Arrange on a tray and enjoy!

(30) Hogwarts Sliders and Potter Patties

This simple yet delicious dish can fit in the palm of your hand! Keep it a secret or share it with others. Eat them alone or with your sister and brothers. Keep it plain or stack them high. They can be eaten day or night.

As with spells and many other objects in the magical world, Hogwarts Sliders and Potter Patties can be topped and used in many different ways.

Ingredient List:

- 1 ½ lb. meat of your choice, ground
- 16 mini slider buns
- Salt
- Pepper
- 1 head of lettuce
- 4 tomatoes, sliced
- Ketchup
- Mayo
- Pickles

HHHHHHHHHHHHHHHHHHHHHHHHHHHHHHHHHHHHHHHHHH

How to Cook:

Arrange buns on a serving platter, set aside.

Place meat in a large bowl and season with salt and pepper, mix till incorporated.

Divide meat into 16 mini sliders.

Cook on skillet/grill until cooked all the way through, approx. 3 minutes per side.

Remove from skillet/grill and let sit on a plate for a couple of minutes (this allows the meat to retain the juices and the flavor).

Place one patty between each slider and top with lettuce, tomato, pickles, ketchup, and mayo.

Serve and enjoy!

Magical Dessert Recipes

HHHHHHHHHHHHHHHHHHHHHHHHHHHHHHHHHHHHHHHHHH

(31) Dumbledore's Pensieve

A Pensieve is a bowl used to hold memories. Once put into the bowl, the memories can be reviewed from an outsider's point of view. Pensieve's are rare and only used by the strongest wizards.

Ingredient List:

- 8 oz Cool Whip
- 1 3oz box blue Jello
- Blue food coloring
- Piping bag

HHHHHHHHHHHHHHHHHHHHHHHHHHHHHHHHHHHHHHHHHH

How to Cook:

Making jello according to package instructions, set aside to cool in a medium to a large bowl.

Add a few drops of blue food coloring to the Cool Whip and stir to create a marbled effect.

Put Cool Whip in a piping bag and use a wide tip.

Cut a spiral in the jello, starting at the center and working your way to the edge.

Using the piping bag, go back in and pipe in the Cool Whip along with the spiral cut.

Let chill in the refrigerator for 1 hour.

Relive your most important memories and enjoy!

(32) Mandrake Pots

A plant used to reverse transfiguration or curses to return people to their natural state. They must be handled carefully as their scream can be deadly.

Ingredient List:

- 1 box chocolate cake mix
- 1 tub chocolate frosting
- Chocolate sprinkles
- Brown or silver cupcake wrappers
- 24 mini ceramic pots
- 24 miniature plastic baby dolls (can be found at craft stores)
- 24 small sticks of parsley

HHHHHHHHHHHHHHHHHHHHHHHHHHHHHHHHHHHHHHHHHH

How to Cook:

Bake cupcakes according to instructions on the box, allow them to cool completely.

Top all cupcakes with icing and chocolate sprinkles.

Push 1 miniature plastic baby doll halfway into the center of each cupcake.

Add in 1 stick of parsley behind each cupcake (this will be the plant).

Optional- to buy small plastic branches/leaves from the craft store and super glue pieces onto the babies' heads.

Enjoy your nursery full of Mandrakes!

(33) Basilisk Dessert

The Basilik is a giant snake that is let loose from the Chamber of Secrets by Tom Riddle (Heir of Slytherin) and set loose in Hogwarts. Looking a Basilisk in the eye immediately killed the victim. During the Chamber of Secrets, several students are petrified because they looked indirectly at the basilisk (via water, a looking glass, etc.). Spiders are deeply afraid of the basilisk, but Argog helps Harry and Ron solve the mystery of who opened the Chamber.

Ingredient List:

- 2 packs large marshmallows
- 2 sticks butter, cut into 1 tablespoon pieces
- 12 cups Kelloggs Rice Krispies (about 2 boxes)
- 2 teaspoons vanilla extract
- Green Food Coloring
- 1 red Twizzler
- Small black cake decorating gel
- *Make in 2 sets so it can be easy to stir*

HHHHHHHHHHHHHHHHHHHHHHHHHHHHHHHHHHHHHHHHHH

How to Cook:

Melt 1 stick of butter in a large pot (DON'T LET IT BURN).

Add 1 pack of marshmallows to the pot, stir till melted.

As soon as marshmallows are melted, add 4 drops of green food coloring and 1 teaspoon vanilla extract.

Stir 6 cups Rice Krispies until incorporated.

Allow to cool for 1 minute and then remove and start forming into the half of a long snake body.

Repeat Steps 1-6 with the second set of ingredients; the first half of the snake body needs to include an oval end for the head, and the second half needs to include a tail portion.

Stick two halves of the snake body together.

Cut Twizzler in half and split one of the ends into a "V" shape.

Lightly push Twizzler into the head portion to form the tongue.

Use black cake decorating gel to draw two eyes on the head and any patterns along the body.

Enjoy!

(34) Treacle Tarte

A very traditional English tart that is generally topped with a dollop of cream. It is a favorite of Harry, and we are first introduced to it in the first book/film Harry and Sorcerer's Stone.

Ingredient List:

- *Store bought pie crust can be used as well*
- 2 cups flour
- 1 stick unsalted butter
- 3 ½ tablespoons cold water
- 1 ¾ cup golden syrup
- ¾ cup breadcrumbs
- 4 tablespoons lemon juice
- Zest of 2 lemons
- 1 egg

HHHHHHHHHHHHHHHHHHHHHHHHHHHHHHHHHHHHHHHHHH

How to Cook:

Add flour and butter to a mixing bowl, combine with your fingers until the texture is very granular (i.e., like sand).

Add water mix until it forms a dough (If the dough is too dry, add water 1 teaspoon at a time).

Wrap dough in plastic wrap and allow to set in the refrigerator for 0.5-1 hour.

Heat oven to 375°F.

Divide the dough into two sections, leave half in the refrigerator.

Roll out the first half of the dough until it is approx. ¼ inch thick.

Place dough in a greased pie tin, press into the side of the pie tie, trim off any excess around the edges.

Gently poke a few spots on the base of the pie crust and place them back in the refrigerator.

In a saucepan, add the golden syrup and heat on low until warm.

Add in breadcrumbs, lemon juice, and lemon zest, stir until well mixed.

Remove the prepared pie tin from the refrigerator and pour the golden syrup mixture into the pie tin.

Remove the second half of dough and roll out on the counter until it is approx. ¼ inch thick.

Cut ½ in strips into the dough and arrange in a lattice design on top of the pie.

Press edges together and brush crust with egg wash.

Bake for 35-40 minutes, or until golden brown.

Let cool for 10 minutes before serving.

Enjoy!

(35) Luna Lovegood Dipped Apples

Luna Lovegood, introduced in the movie/book 5 Order of the Phoenix, belongs to the Ravenclaw House. She is tough to be strange to most other students. She is unique and didn't seem to care what others thought of her. She could see Nargles and was always looking for her shoes.

Ingredient List:

- 12 Granny Smith apples
- 12 wooden apple sticks
- Bag of caramel
- Toppings: Sprinkles, nuts, M&Ms, Oreos, etc.
- *Optional- Bag of melting chocolate

HHHHHHHHHHHHHHHHHHHHHHHHHHHHHHHHHHHHHHHHH

How to Cook:

Wash and dry apples.

Push 1 wooden apple sticks halfway into each apple, set it aside.

Melt caramel in short intervals in the microwave, stirring in between.

One at a time, dip apples into caramel and let excess drip off.

Sprinkle toppings onto each apple (DO NOT roll apple in sprinkles as the caramel may come off).

Allow apple to set on a piece of parchment paper (place the apple in the microwave will speed up this process).

Enjoy your fun orchard!

**The melting chocolate can be substituted for the caramel, or you can do half the apples with caramel and the other half with chocolate.*

(36) Monster Book Treats

Hagrid gifted a required book for all Third Years, Harry his copy. The book contains what you need to know about taking care of magical creatures, but the book is highly volatile and often attacks whoever is trying to read it. When Harry opens his copy, the book tries to attack his hand, and Harry Uses a belt to keep it shut.

Ingredient List:

- 1 box of Graham Crackers
- 1 bag of mini-marshmallows
- 1 tub chocolate frosting
- Colored M&Ms

HHHHHHHHHHHHHHHHHHHHHHHHHHHHHHHHHHHHHHHH

How to Cook:

Break Graham Crackers in half and arrange on a serving tray (12 crackers would equal 24 halves).

Ice one side of the cracker and top with a mini-marshmallows

Ice the other side of the cracker and place, frosting side up on top of the marshmallows (think marshmallow sandwich).

Arrange 6 M&M eyes in the center of the frosting.

Repeat until all Graham Crackers have been used up.

Enjoy your ravenous library!

(37) Chocolate Frogs

We first encounter a chocolate frog on Harry's first train ride to Hogwarts. The frogs come in a special box with collectible cards. The frogs have about one good jump in them. Harry's first collectible card is Albus Dumbledore, but his frog jumps out the window before eating it.

Ingredient List:

- Chocolate frog mold (from a local craft store)
- 1-2 lbs. melting chocolate

HHHHHHHHHHHHHHHHHHHHHHHHHHHHHHHHHHHHHHHHHH

How to Cook:

Melt chocolate according to package directions (can be done on the stove or in the microwave).

Pour just enough chocolate into frog molds to coat the molds but not fill them up.

Place molds in the freezer for approx. 3 minutes, or until hardened.

Repeat steps 1-3 until the entire mold is filled.

Once the final amount of chocolate has been added and frozen, flip the frog mold over and lightly tap chocolate pieces out.

Jump for joy and eat some frogs!

(38) Acid Pops

One of most popular treats sold at Honeydukes in Hogsmead. Though they were very sweet and tasty, they had a nasty trick of burning a hole in the tongue.

Ingredient List:

- 12 lollipops (Tootsie Rolls pops work great)
- ½ cup honey
- 6 packages of different colored pop rocks
- Piece of Styrofoam (for displaying cake pops)

How to Cook:

Pour pop rocks into individual bowls (by color)

Unwrap lollipops and stick in Styrofoam

Using a small bowl, warm honey microwave for 30 seconds

One by one, dip each lollipop in the honey and then roll in the pop rocks

Surprise your guests and enjoy!

(39) Golden Snitch Pops

The goal of all quidditch tournaments is to catch the golden snitch. Whoever catches the golden snitch automatically wins the tournament!

Ingredient List:

- 1 box cake mix (can be any flavor)
- 1 container vanilla frosting
- 6 small containers of gold sprinkles
- Yellow melting chocolate
- White Fondant
- Lollipop sticks
- Long piece of Styrofoam (for drying/displaying cake pops)

HHHHHHHHHHHHHHHHHHHHHHHHHHHHHHHHHHHHHHHH

How to Cook:

Bake cake according to instructions on the box, allow the cake to cool completely.

Pour gold sprinkles on a plate and set them aside.

Once the cake is cool, crumble into a large bowl.

Add in a tub of vanilla frosting and mix with your hands.

Scoop out 3-4 tablespoons-sized portions and roll into balls (think slightly smaller than a golf ball), and you should be able to make approx. 35-50 cake balls.

Line cake balls on a cookie sheet and place them in the refrigerator for a couple of hours (this allows them to stay compact during the rest of the recipe).

Melt the yellow chocolate in the microwave (see package directions for melting details).

Insert one lollipop stick into each cake ball.

Carefully dip each cake pop into the yellow melting chocolate and immediately roll in gold sprinkles.

Stick each cake pop in the Styrofoam piece to dry.

Once all cake pops are made, roll out white fondant.

Cut long thin triangle pieces in the fondant, making little feather marks on each piece.

Attach triangles to the side of the cake pops by reheating leftover melting chocolate and using a small dot as "glue" to attach the wings.

Enjoy your match and may the best player win!

(40) Sorting Hat Cupcakes

One of the most famous objects in Harry was The Sorting Hat. Containing the intelligence of the four founders, The Sorting Hat was placed on First Year's heads and able to see into their magical capabilities. It would use its mastery of Legilimency to sort the First Years into their houses.

Ingredient List:

- 1 box yellow or white cake mix
- 12 red M&Ms
- 12 green M&Ms
- 12 yellow M&Ms
- 12 blue M&Ms
- 1 tub white or chocolate frosting
- 24 Hershey's Kisses
- 12 Oreos, halved and filling removed
- ½ cup brown melting chocolate
- Gold star sprinkles
- Gold cupcake wrappers
- Piping bag with a wide tip

HHHHHHHHHHHHHHHHHHHHHHHHHHHHHHHHHHHHHHHH

How to Cook:

Bake cupcakes according to instructions on the box, except placing 2 M&Ms of the same color inside before baking.

Allow cupcakes to cool completely before decorating.

Remove the wrapper from Hershey's Kisses and set it aside.

Spoon frosting into the piping bag.

Melt ½ cup chocolate in the microwave.

Secure a Hershey's Kiss to each Oreo half using a small amount (1/2 teaspoons) or melted chocolate, set aside.

Pipe frosting onto each cupcake but leave a small portion of the cupcake still visible.

Gently place one Oreo cookie onto the top of the frosted cupcakes.

Sprinkle gold stars onto the top of each cupcake.

Enjoy finding out which house you are sorted into!

Author's Afterthoughts

THANK YOU

You will not regret your choice to buy my book and read it from beginning to end! Thank you for taking precious time out of your day to peruse my work and try a recipe or two. My hope is that you find benefit within its pages and your culinary skills progress beyond the content.

There is an overwhelming variety of choices in the world today, so the fact that you considered your options and decided to take a chance on my work fills me with gratitude.

Fill in an online review on Amazon and let me know what you thought! Don't hold back, I want your honest opinion. Others will benefit from your experience and I will get the necessary feedback I need to create better books in the future!

Thank you,

PD. Morgan

Printed in Great Britain
by Amazon

32818711R00064